NAIVE BUTTERFLIES

You know when you meet someone for the first time, and you can just tell there a good person and they have so much love in their heart.

That's how Momma T made everyone feel.

There was never a question or even a though as to how much she loved every single person.

In all my years I've never met someone who made me genuinely feel like it was ok to not only be myself, but to put myself first.

Momma T was one of the only lights in my life for a long time.

I will always cherish her kindness, her jokes, and willingness to be a star in the dark sky on any given day.

I will spend every day of my life trying to be even half as incredible as you were.

Thank you for teaching me what it's like to be a role model.

Every summer day when I walk outside and see the overgrown green grass blowing in the wind, butterflies dancing around the wildflowers, and wind chimes singing in the background. I will think of you.

When I look up at the stars and see the brightest one. I will think of you

In Loving memory of Amy S. Teeter.

For those who have the part time job of keeping everyone happy. Thinking of every outcome before the conversation has even begun so you can control it and keep the peace. Because somehow, it always seems to be our fault.

For all the nights I stayed up with nobody to talk to.

For all the sad days where anxiety told me I was the problem instead of those around me.

For all the fun times that were ruined by the past or present that crept into the moment.

And for me.

Sometimes playing dumb is the only way to survive.

For those who choose to underestimate the lowest player will always fall short of the intelligence of those who read the room to play the game.

Welcome to my head of Naïve Butterflies.

You know that feeling when sadness washes over you?
That empty void of nothing that rolls into the back of your mind and takes over.
It doesn't matter where you are, who you're with, or how much fun you're having.
It comes rolling in like a thunderstorm but feels like the calm before the storm.
Where the wind, and rain stop.
That eerie lingering feeling of panic wondering when the storm is going to hit.
That's how I feel all the time. That's just how it's always been.
Waiting...
Lingering...
Wondering when the next terrible thing is going to happen or what I can do to stop it.
Truth be told there's nothing you can do.
Nothing you can say.
There's no preparation you can do to prepare for what is going to happen.
And if there's anything I've learned it's that no matter what happens. Things can always get worse

All the warnings in the world couldn't prepare me

for the bag of tricks, you had up your sleeve

to try and ruin me.

There's not enough paper, time, or energy in the world for me to be able to write down all the times you've disappointed me.

I didn't realize that maybe the cause of all my loss was me

Maybe this whole time while I was pointing fingers at those who tried to kill me before

I should have been writing the truth

I only had to look in the mirror

I could have stared the killer in the face

In my face

I would have realized maybe I was hurting myself the whole time

Or maybe that's just what they wanted me to think..

Sometimes I wonder how you don't see it

Did you blind yourself from the memories?

For if I looked into the mirror and saw you
staring back at me

I would run too

And never come back.

Home is a safe place, that's what they'll tell you.

Home is where the heart is. Home is where you

feel happy. But what if, I haven't felt safe, happy,

or real in a very long time.

I just feel like I'm going to be stuck forever like no matter how hard I try and show myself off.

I.

will always be.

Stuck.

in the inner motions of not

being enough.

There are days where I just want someone to receive the love I give.

There are years where I just wanted one ounce of hope.

One ounce of interest.

But would that be too much?

Would that drain you of your thirst for me?

I sit amongst a sea of people as a fraud

As a liar

For I know nothing about love

But I envy love

I romanticize my life even though love has never come to stay

But gently breezed by me

Taunting me

Just enough to keep me wishing

That one day

Maybe some day

I could be worthy of its touch

Maybe I should be like the rain

as if all the emotion ....
could drop down everywhere touching everything
in its path.

But what if I Drench someone with my sorrow

What if I flood the world?

What if the flood is too big?

When all the emotions mix together in the flood,
will I continue to feel so much that I feel nothing
at all?

You said I was the Apple of your eye,

but what happened?

You left.

Leaving me to rot.

I wanted to be swallowed into the earth

To decompose

But per usual I had to

Fight.

Fight off the worms, the birds, and everything
that tried to pick me apart.

I haven't stopped fighting since you left, but the
day you left.
You stopped fighting.

I no longer stay on the ground.

waiting to be treated like the fresh fruit you
wanted me so badly to be.

But I won't change for you

I'll make my own way.

Because nothing is ever good enough for you

Nobody will ever be good enough for you except
yourself

So, I killed all the fresh fruit

I'm worthy now, even if you left me and forgot
about me like you did everything else

I sat under the weeping willow tree begging
someone to find me.

I'm lost

I'm tired

and I'm hurt

I need someone to help me understand.

Help me understand how this happened.

Help me understand how that place is supposed
to make me into a better person.

Help me understand why she left last night.

Help me understand why I can't do anything
right.

Why does everyone see straight through my pleading attempt for love.

Like a two-way mirror but nobody's looking in

I can only see out

Why am I so invisible....

Sometimes when I hear people yelling, I go down memory lane.

I reminisce in the high-pitched voices

They are just background noise for the mental images and videos I have reeling in my brain

But that's memory lane for you

The paradox

that just so happens to be the worst part of my life.

Don't talk when the adults are talking.

I never get to speak.

Like a muzzle

I had nobody.

Just me myself and I.

And I barely had myself.

At war with the way they treated each other.

I just wanted to be heard.

I wanted to be seen.

I've been silenced.

Easter is ruined.

It will never be the same.

"Choose" she said.

Him or me.

Vacation is what popped into the 8 year old girls mind.

Family dinner or vacation?

Vacation sounds good

The only vacation I took that day was the baggage that went on the trip.

We never went back

you didn't come back either.

That's the day I lost you even if you act like you
don't remember

I tried to pack you in my suitcase, but you didn't
want to fit.

You chose not to.

To be on high alert for your whole life?

Feels like you're walking on wet paint trying not
to get it on your feet.

But on the other hand, your trying not to slide
across the floor

But you will always falling short of doing the
impossible

Because how can you walk across the wet paint
without getting it on your feet?

You can't

"Hug your sister" my grandma said.

I stood there
mouth wide open
like she had finally lost her marbles

You're crazy

I'm an only child

or was that a lie too.

Another secret they kept from me.

Another?
 How fun?
  How scary?
  How?
    How I wish they never let you in.

How nobody will ever know the things you did.

For I'll never say them outloud.

I was scared.

Terrified.

Not only of the home I lived in but those who lived in the home.

They were abusive.

They used me.

Like a pawn.

A prize.

Some people will throw you into the wall like a
wineglass during a bad argument

they don't care if you
break,
chip,
or shatter.

They will expect you to hold it together while
they fix themselves, so you do.

You stay and listen why they fill you with

their problems, liquid falls through the cracks, but
you better catch every drop. You're expected to

but never ask for anything in return because that
would be too much to ask for

After all you're just a broken wine glass, not even
on sale for full price.

You left me so easily

so fast

Like a person filling up their car at a gas station.

You took what you needed from me and left.

Left me there waiting for somebody else to come along and use me again.

Hoping that maybe one day.

It will be the same as it once was.

Accept the gas station closed,

and never opened back up

Leaving me behind,

with nobody to use me anymore like you did.

Alone.

Forever.

With a gap so ghastly deep that I can never fill.

For nobody deserves to be let in like I let you.

And if you ever take a walk down memory lane
with me in mind

I hope you think about all the time and energy

I put into this something that just wasn't meant
to be.

I hope you'll think about all the things I planned

and all the things that we could've been.

I hope you'll think to the times when I was there
and nobody else was to be seen.

And finally

I hope you'll finally appreciate all the time and effort I put in the same thing that just.

wasn't

giving anything back.

A one-sided battle

Please don't go.

Thermostat punched

Car dented.

Crushed.

so mean.

so violent.

She didn't even touch you....

You were so angry.

You always chose violence.

You were violence.

You were the problem.

You never had our best intentions at heart.

You only had your own.

I am broken.

Like the thermostat you punched off the wall.

Unlike the thermostat

I never had the chance to be fixed.

I never had the chance to keep you.

But like the thermostat

I watched you go from hot to cold

like I didn't matter. Because I didn't.

Maybe if you spent more time with your me than you did inside that.. that place.

 Thing's would have turned out different.

but you didn't.

you chose the "better" path.

You chose the easy path.

 A coward

Minutes turned into lightyears and words turned to distant encouragement.

I could have loved you.

We could have taken over the world.

I wouldn't have to watch your life in distant solitude.

You wouldn't have to stay away.

But things weren't meant to be for us.

You made sure of that.

I just want you to know you missed out on

A great child.
A great girl.
A great teenager.
A great woman.

You could have walked me down the isle.

On my wedding day....

You could have loved me, but you chose not too.

I miss you, but this isn't fair to me.

I've spent most of my trips around the sun living with this weight inside of me.

A weight that's there because of you.

I tried to forget you.

I tried to press the thought of you down until you were nothing but a distant memory and for a while

I thought it worked.

But now

I'm falling in love with life.
With my passions.

And that made me realize just how much damage you did to my heart.

I can't live with this pain anymore.

I can't carry around this sadness because it's
stopping me from being the person I want to be.

I can't be that person if I am constantly wondering what I did wrong,

why you let me go and decided you didn't want to be my football throwing buddy anymore.

So, I forgive you.

Because there is no longer a you.

My next chapter doesn't concern you and the only person you can thank is yourself.

"Go live with him then" she said.

I never knew how much hurt could come from something so simple.

So forward.

She didn't want me.

For I was too much for her.

I'm always TOO MUCH

A simple task that yells out for one's attention.

It's simple.

Can't you see? It's simple honey, can't you see.

Can't you see!?

You can't do anything right Kaitlin.

why

Why

Why can't you be perfect.

Why can't you please everyone.

WHY can't you choose me to make him upset.

WHY Kaitlin why can't you just do one thing right.

Why are you even here if you can't be in a million different correct places at once?

Damn

You're useless

You never let me be free,

you kept me in a cage.

If I dared to be myself,

If I dared to be me

Heaven forbid there's a flaw in my code.

So keep the flaws coming.

Because without them you can't scream and
yell….
And we all know YOU love to scream and yell.

Trying to please you is like trying to glue a
never-ending cracked tunnel.

A cyclone trying to wrap its arms around me and
crush me under the constant pressure

that I'm never up to your standards.

A constant WEIGHT of pressure.

Maybe it's me putting it all on myself,

maybe I'm the problem.

No.

That's exactly what they want you to think.

That they love you and they could never do
wrong.

Their lying.

Was it to much?
Was I too much ?
Was it the way I. Seven year old me patched you together?
I couldn't patch the holes in the wall.

But I could fix you.

I thought I could fix you.

Turns out you became an even bigger disappointment

 The relationship we once had is something I will hold dear to my heart.

You chose superficial items over me.

You chose you over me.

You chose anything over me.

Rain not only brings joy to a young girl who will soon know great sadness and disappointment, but happiness.

Friends ?
What?
She finally made friends ?

It doesn't matter that they're seniors and you're in seventh grade, right?

 Friends?

Oh how a eight lettered phrase changed who you thought you were going to be.

Oh how a word put such a dark and unforeseen sorrow

In the storm drain that day.

Oh how if only you could have stopped the rain.
The worst days of my life.
Happen in my favorite thing

RAIN

They said you would never be with a girl like me.

They said a girl like me could never have a guy
like you.

You said they were crazy.

how I wished I had listened.

How I wish I stayed in my room.

You said they were jealous.

And who was I?

But trying to make you happy?

You were supposed to be there.

But you forgot about me.

Now, I'm terrified of storm drains

What have I done wrong?
What is it that I have done to deserve to
deteriorate in this hell while I call it my safe
haven.

I am never safe.

I never will be safe.

For I Will Always Be On The Run

The only person I had left

In an o so lonely world

Danced

on the broken pieces of my heart with

no mercy to the owner.

Am I supposed to feel bad about the connection
that once lit up so bright like a kid on Christmas
is now

A flickering light.

Because you did this. You stomped out all the
light in my life, and covered my world with a
darkness I've never known

I only knew light until you ripped the switch out
of the wall.

Your path?

you can either accept it for what it is

or you can fight it

and go after it

and knock down whatever comes in the way.

I recommend you always fight.. when the time is right.

I let you beat me with your words and your
actions

because I thought it was better to be your friend
than to be

the fat girl with no friends.

You made sure I knew you were better than me.

You were the queen.
You looked better than me.
You got all the guys.
You stole my "real" friends
You used me.

You won the race every day.

I made sure of it.

Because if you left.. you would take everything
and everyone I cared about. And we both know
you would take my will to live too.

You made a fool out of me for seven years.
But

Who's the fool now?

How's that relationship going by the way?
Yeah..

That's what I thought

I used to feel like a boat,

always trying to go with the water.

Having the weight of the sea of opinions push my boat in the right direction.

Now I feel like the wind in the sail,

I can go in whatever direction at whatever given moment.

It's moment like these I find hope...... but then that feeling comes back.

I'm so tired of people looking through me.

Telling me who I am.

Reading me. Like they know me?

Like my shoes are on their feet.

Telling me what I am.

I will NEVER change for anyone again.

You don't know me.. Nobody does.

This is where everything changed.

For the better.

For the worst.

And for me.

The invisibility of a person who lets people run over her is gone.

She's found people who make her feel different in the best way.

They don't say she's too loud or too much.

But accept her for who she is.

They understand her.

That's foreign.

The minute you stop and actually feel the rain
instead of running through it.

Is the moment you live.

That moment where you realize things are a lot
bigger than
"am I good enough"
"am I skinny enough"
"am I strong enough"
or
" am I too fat"
It's the day you change.

See, in the grand scheme of things.

None of that stuff matters.

You're going to get to where you're going no
matter what.

Love?

What is love?

That's the simple question I've been asking myself with every season.

Is love sticking around for the people who treat you like the last piece of bread nobody wants?

Is love like it appears in the fairy tales?

Is love selfish?

Is love supposed to be one generalized thing?

No

Love is hard.
Love is simple.

Love is a double sided sword.

Love is tough.
But love is also sweet.

There's no definition of love.

Just like there's no definition of you.

Love is a power of great evil.

Love takes all strong asset's and de weaponizes
them.

All the time and effort.

ALL the work you've done to build yourself up.

All the night's you spent alone by choice to try
and prove to yourself you don't need anyone.

That you are better off alone.

It takes them all and hit's the BIG red heart
shaped detonation button that specifically says

"DO NOT PUSH"

And destroys everything in its reach.

I once had a shot at love.

Or what I thought was love.

But like all great things in the wind.
It flew away

And didn't put up a fight.

I spend every aspect and breath of my existence

daydreaming of a love that is built and critiqued

to my perfect fantasy.

Planning every conversation, activity, and
scenario.

So, I won't be the cause of my own vanity.

Again.

I loved you with everything I was.

But the universe wasn't ready.

And neither was I.

For you never wanted our stars to align.

Or even be in the same galaxy.

When I was asked about love as a teenager I
always said "I've never been in love"

but that's not true.

I've been in love a couple of times.

But after each love I was left more broken than
the one before.

But it's easier to act as if I've never known love,
than to re-live you.

I was a monster in my own head, for who would ever look at me and see a light so bright it hurt their eyes.

So, I became the darkness.

But when the darkness creeped in like the tide on a summer night, I embraced the flood. For it made me feel whole

I fell more in love with sadness than myself.

For sadness has never left me

But I have lost myself over and over again

The relationship we once had is something I will hold dear to my heart.

You used me for your own personal boost in life.

A jumpstart

For a long time, it felt like no matter who I was or what I did.

That I was doing it wrong.

I tried to figure out what was wrong with me.

And when I couldn't figure it out

I tried to be more like "likeable" people.

Changing my personality so people would like me.

The hardest realization I've ever had to face.

It wasn't me.

It was everyone else.

I'd like to think that if we never speak again.

You would look back and realize,

How all the wonders of the world are still waiting
for you.
How all the labyrinths are waiting to be solved,
and how all that makes you curious is waiting to
be told.

There's a lot of light and dark in this world, and
even though sometimes the dark might outweigh
everything.

I hope you never see a world that's not full of
light.

Because even though you don't care, I still love
you.

I think I realized I needed to do some damage control when I longed for peace.

Dreamed of peace.

When all I could think about is happiness.

But I didn't know what I was looking for

I had never experienced peace

But heard about it in the movies

How would I describe our friendship?

If you're a tire going 90 mph on the interstate,
and we hit a feather.

The tire would burst

like the inconspicuous tendencies of someone
who just doesn't care about anybody but
themselves.

I've never met anyone who hurts me to my core
like you do.

I never allowed anyone to get that close.

But I made an acceptation for you.

Because I thought you were one of a kind.

Turns out your just like the rest of them

A maniac disguised as the feeling of comfort

Turns out you're just someone who makes empty promises you know won't come true, because you never plan to act on them.

When all the bridges have been burned, and all the rope is in Knotts with the lies you told.

Who will save you?

Will you look around and miss me?

Or is isolation what you want?

I'll give you a knife.

To cut through the rope and find your way back to me.

But the sad part is

I don't think you'd pick up the knife.

I know I'm not the one you really want.

You settled because you were scared.

Scared that I was the last option for you.

You were just scared to be alone.

You used me.
You lied to me.

You disappoint me.

Let go of the illusion he has any intention of becoming better for you.

Have his intentions ever changed.

Exactly

I like to daydream.

Some days I rather spend most of my time in my head.

Making my perfect world.

A world where I'm not a version of myself that everyone else wants me to be.

But maybe and just maybe. I'm happy.

If I knew I would have gotten myself tangled in your strings of complexity.

I would have never fought for your attention.

They say the worst thing a girl can do is get in her head.

But what if that's the only place where I truly feel safe.

You got into my head plenty of times

You broke into the only place I had for only me.

And left me screaming in more pain with every visit,

You lit the fire and told me to put it out
But you handed me lighter fluid and locked me in
a maze of mirrors

trying to figure out how to set myself free.

Even with your best intentions, my soul lays
thrown about.
Even with your worst intentions I still love you.

Isn't that a problem

Isn't that pathetic

Looking for meaning in all the little nothing's of
the world adds a hint of
Magic
to even the most mediocre of days.

Trying to find signs that you're in the right place.

Searching in
   Billboards
      Books
         License plates
           Coffee shops
         Thin air
            Your eyes

For my nature is to explore and find peace

Maybe it's the way you laugh at the same things I laugh at.
Maybe it's the way you look at me when I make a joke that's just not that funny.
Or maybe it's the way you make me feel like I have purpose in the world without the judgement of wisdom flowing off your soul.

I like it here.

One day I woke up and realized that I couldn't continue living the way I was.

I love myself,

And if the people around me don't fall in love with the real me.

Then they never really loved me to start.

Regret is the invisible cloak of what remains of the choices we wish we made.

Even if nobody cares.

I want to dance in the rain
    I want to do donuts in the parking lot.
I want to go to the movies by myself.
    I want to read books in a coffee shop.
I want to throw big parties and get wasted.
    I want to wake up early.
I want to stay up all night.
    I want to write until my hands hurt.
I want to scream until my throat is raw.
    I want to make a change.
I want to listen to Taylor Swift at full volume.
    I want to go on spontaneous trips.
I want to inspire.
    I want to laugh.
I want to make beautiful things.
    I want to adopt kids.
I want to get married.
    I want to be your hype man.
I want to hold you while you cry.

I want to live a life so wonderful that it makes
people wonder if I'm real.

You are always one step away from the life
you've always wanted.

Take it.

The only thing in your way is air.

Or yourself..

Even when someone cut's you so deep it makes
you think you will never love or be loved again.

Remember.

Embrace the uncertainty.

Because only you can decide if and when your
heart is ready to find someone who moves you.

Surround yourself with the absolute one hundred
percent truth.

Remember that all it takes is a thought and a
spark of love

If one day you wake up different.

Don't be scared.
Don't push it down.

You're evolving into something.

And it's up to you to figure out what.

People do not change.

Read that again.

People do not change because you want them too.

They change because they want too.

If they want to. They will

You can't force them.

Go to the energy.

In all aspects of your life.

Even on days you have no energy to give.

Sometimes when you've been through so much pain.

You can't recover.

The only thing you can do is make the courageous decision to turn it into something worthwhile.

The pain will still linger. Waiting for you to slip up

You just have to come to terms with it, and follow the energy to recover your own happiness.

One toxic trait that always comes knocking at my door

in the middle of the night

is learning to stop shrinking myself to fit into lower expectations.

If they didn't love you when you were big

They won't love you when your small.

Sadness creeps into even the biggest moments.

It's ok to acknowledge it.

Because if you don't

It will wait.

And it won't just creep in

It will take over

The funny thing about sadness is it will wait you
out

For sadness waits for
No damsel
 No Man
No woman
 No time

For sadness waits for no body.

I've always thought butterflies were some of the most misunderstood creatures.

Always looked at for their beauty.

Never once looked past for all the important purposes they have.

Because there just pretty to look at.

I think that there's time in every situation to reflect.

To really dive deep and step back and think about all the ways.

one decision.

One sacrifice can have all the positives in your life go straight downhill.

How will you fix it?

How will thing's play out when you need them too.

That's the question.

Life waits for no circumstance or variable.

You will never be fully prepared

You must learn to love yourself

Because although prince charming is real

He is a prince.

Not glue

Prince charming's job isn't to glue you back together.

You have to do that yourself.

It is not my job to alter anything about my art because you don't like the shade.

I have spent my darkest and brightest moments creating this piece of work.

I spent too long critiquing it myself.

I will not let anyone critique it any longer,

Every home I've ever had has been destroyed.

Home is no longer a place

I am my safe place.
I am home

I often play scenarios in my head of what life would have been like if you loved me.

Or how things could have been if you weren't a coward.

If you would have kept loving me

And didn't block me out

Because that's what you did

It was easier to forget I existed than to realize just how evil you were

You were the first villain I ever encountered.

And to think

You were my first hero..

I never knew being friends with you was going to be like playing a game of telephone.

He said she said accept it was just you manipulating information to your own benefit.

I just want you to know that even though were both grown and busy

I miss you, and I love you

I will always be rooting you on

Standing on the sidelines and wishing we could go back to how things used to be.

But we can't.

I hope you know that you saved my life.

I miss our early morning Jam sessions.

I miss our late-night talks before school.

I miss us teaming up and knocking the others off the top bunk.

I miss hearing about your day.

Living in the basement with my best friend is what got me to where I am now.

Thank you for being the only person I had.

I will always cherish that

You are one of the purest human being's I've ever met.

If everyone was like you

The world would be restored.

Nobody would ever long for peace again.

I'm Still on my healing journey…..

But I'm a adult now, and I've learned so much about myself in the past four years.

Dare I say?

To be continued??

A message from the Author.

If you're reading this, I want to thank you from the bottom of my heart. I want you to start putting yourself first. Be selfish for a while. You can choose you, and still be a good person. Repeat that.

There are so many people I hold dear to my heart that deserve the world. They put up with my late-night overthinking, my morning overthinking, and my endless battles with my own mind.
Instead of listing them, I'm just going to say. You know who you are babes!

LOVE you all and thank you for healing with me.

Made in the USA
Columbia, SC
15 July 2023

20102183R00140